SAMUEL BARBER
Early Piano Works

Edited by Richard Walters

ED 4430
First Printing: March 2010

ISBN 978-1-4234-9111-8

G. SCHIRMER, Inc.

DISTRIBUTED BY

 HAL•LEONARD®
CORPORATION
7777 W. BLUEMOUND RD. P.O. BOX 13819 MILWAUKEE, WI 53213

www.schirmer.com
www.halleonard.com

CONTENTS

All are first published editions except *Three Sketches*, published privately in 1924, and *Interlude I.*

PREFACE

Notice to Mother and nobody else

Dear Mother: I have written this to tell you my worrying secret.
Now don't cry when you read it because it is neither yours nor my
fault. I suppose I will have to tell it now without any nonsense. To begin
with I was not meant to be an athlet [sic]. I was meant to be a composer,
and will be I'm sure. I'll ask you one more thing.—Don't ask me to try
to forget this unpleasant thing and go play football.—Please—
Sometimes I've been worrying about this so much that it makes me
mad (not very),

                                                    Love,
                                                    Sam Barber II
                                                    [written at age 9]

Few people are as self-aware of destiny at such a young age as was young Sam Barber. Even at 9-years-old he knew that he was a composer, and also was at least somewhat aware of the insecurities and consequences of an unconventional creative life. He was also a natural pianist. In his early years composition and piano were inseparably linked. In the July 13, 1921 issue of a small Pennsylvania newspaper, the *West Chester Daily Local News*, Samuel Barber's mother stated that her son had been a pianist "since his infancy."[1] By the age of six Barber was improvising at the instrument, and his first fully notated composition, for piano, appeared four months after his seventh birthday. Even though he would become the greatest of American vocal composers, and write expertly for other instruments and the orchestra, Barber's development as a musician and composer can be ascertained in his early works for piano, composed primarily for his own playing, and his early songs for voice and piano. It is with pleasure that we present in this edition, for the first time, Barber's piano pieces composed from age 7 to 21. Through the chronology of pieces in this collection one can see the composer's development, and his embrace of traditional literature by various composers.

Barber shows talent even in childhood compositions, included in this collection in manuscript facsimiles. The short pieces written before the age of twelve, though simple, are complete ideas. His strong sense of melody, which would serve as an anchor to his creative output, was there from the beginning. Though he sometimes imitated sentimental lighter music of the day, the early works show precocious sophistication and sensitivity. The manuscripts from his teen years show a remarkably exacting and mature grasp of music notation.

Born on March 9, 1910 to Dr. Roy Barber and his wife, Daisy, Samuel Osborne Barber II (named after his paternal grandfather) grew up in West Chester, Pennsylvania, 30 miles from Philadelphia. Sam's father had expectations his son would not fulfill. The composer stated, "I was supposed to be a doctor. I was supposed to go to Princeton. And everything I was supposed to do I didn't." Though he played piano (undoubtedly helped by his pianist mother), as is obvious by his compositions for the instrument, formal lessons did not begin until age 9. At that time he began study with local teacher William Hatton Green, a good musician by all counts, until entering the Curtis Institute of Music in Philadelphia at age 14 in September of 1924. But even before his more ambitious musical life began at Curtis, Barber's development as a musician and composer galloped along. Prior to Curtis we know that he had composed 13 piano pieces, 15 songs, one vocal duet, two songs for voice and organ, one piece for chorus with soloists and organ, and an unfinished opera. By age 12 he was a paid organist in West Chester. He was greatly influenced by his aunt, Louise Homer, a professional singer at the Metropolitan Opera, and her husband, Sidney Homer, a composer. Both were encouraging mentors throughout his youth. Aunt Louise sang many early Barber songs for him, and sometime later also in public. Uncle Sidney was an interested and informal composition teacher to the boy.

Barber was in the first class to enter the newly formed Curtis Institute of Music. He remained a student at West Chester High School, and traveled to Philadelphia and to Curtis at least one day each week. By all accounts Sam was a star student at Curtis. Beyond talent and enthusiasm, he possessed natural charisma and energy at this young age. Besides composition, he studied piano and voice there. Piano studies were first with George Boyle, followed by five years of study with Isabelle Vengerova, a legendary teacher whose piano students later included Leonard Bernstein, Lukas Foss, Leonard Pennario, Gary Graffman and Abbey Simon. Barber's composition and theory teacher, Rosario Scalero, was his most far-reaching influence. With Scalero for nine years, Barber studied in a very thorough, traditional European approach. Barber's love of Europe and its music, languages, poetry and art, so evident in his works, was cemented with his first summer there, at the age of 18. He would return many times.

For various reasons Barber chose not to publish these early works. He was always self-critical, and particularly so of the music he composed in the pre-Curtis and Curtis years. Nevertheless, he did save these early pieces throughout his life, so they clearly meant something to him. At this writing, nearly 30 years after his death (January 23, 1981), and 100 years since his birth, it seems appropriate to consider the historical worth of the entire output of such a major American composer. And certainly it is worthwhile to consider the natural, expressive talents of the boy composer Sam Barber in seeking the source of his later great works. The capturing of sincerely felt emotion, the melodic gift, spontaneity, and a deep sense of natural harmony are qualities found in all his works, early and late.

The only known piano pieces left unpublished are exercises composed for Scalero while at Curtis. These are various counterpoint assignments, and though interesting for some of Barber's creative touches, are pedagogical in purpose. In our judgment they were not appropriate for inclusion in this edition.

Though not a concert artist, Barber was an accomplished and naturally talented pianist. The most notable evidences of this are his song recordings with Leontyne Price. As a collaborator his touch is both sensitive and strong. A vivid musical personality is revealed in these recordings. One especially notes his directional sense of lyrical phrase, but without sentimentality.

For a personal glimpse of Barber as a creative personality, perhaps Paul Wittke, Barber's editor at G. Schirmer for decades, said it best. "Barber rarely discussed his own music (a modesty alien to most composers); if he did, he made sport of it, although he was ferociously proud of it. I always felt that he thought he never measured up to his own expectations or exacting standards. No one could."[3]

There are too few published references about Samuel Barber. I am indebted to Barbara Heyman's definitive research on the topic. My thanks to those who supplied manuscript sources for research from the Library of Congress, Eastman School of Music, and West Chester County Historical Society. I also wish to thank Joshua Parman, Joel Boyd, David Flachs and Laura Ward for their contributions to this edition.

Richard Walters
editor

NOTES ON THE MUSIC

In chronological order of composition.

Themes
"Op. X, No. 2." Composed in April, 1923. These pieces are the first teenage compositions that clearly indicate Barber's continued mastery of the piano as a player and composer, and his growing discovery of piano literature. Barber later disregarded the opus number assigned in boyhood. Previously unpublished. Source: Chester County Historical Society.

I. Menuetto
Barber composed a different and longer version of this minuet for *Three Sketches*. He also arranged this minuet for vocal duet with piano accompaniment.

II. Andante Religioso
Besides the influence of perhaps Schumann, Barber seems to be discovering harmonic color and voice leading in a new way.

III. Allegretto on C
The composition date on this movement is 1920. Barber later worked the same material in a 1924 composition, *Fantasie for Two Pianos in the Style of Josef Haydn.*

Petite Berceuse
Composed *c*1923. The manuscript was later recopied. The melody is songlike and has a folk flavor. Though rather sentimental, the piece has an elegant simplicity. The dedication "To Jean" was added after Barber began study at the Curtis Institute of Music in 1924, when he may have dedicated the piece to Jeanne Behrend, a friend and fellow student of composition and piano who often played his music.[2] Previously unpublished. Source: Chester County Historical Society.

Three Sketches
The set, *Three Sketches for Pianoforte*, was published by Barber's father in a private edition, 1924. This in itself indicates the young composer's sense of accomplishment in these pieces. As with the *Themes* of the previous year, Barber's discovery of piano literature and his maturing fluency as a composer is evident. Source: Chester County Historical Society.

I. Love Song
Composed in April, 1924. Published in *American Composers of the Twentieth Century* (Schaum, 1969), and later as a single sheet published by Alfred. Barber dedicated "Love Song" to his mother. The piece has a natural flow and melody, as well as restrained elegance in the style of lighter music Barber encountered. In measure 16 in the left hand one guesses that the grace notes are a possible mistake, and might be correctly spelled E F rather than F G.

II. To My Steinway
Composed in June, 1923. Barber's dedication is to the manufacturing edition number of his Steinway, "To Number 230601." His tender regard for the piano, and to piano literature the piece echoes, is obvious.

III. Minuet
Composed in April, 1923. Barber borrowed a theme from Beethoven's "Minuet in G Major" in the piece, which he cited on the manuscript. This is the composer's most ambitious piano composition to date.

Fantasie for Two Pianos
Written in the Style of Josef Haydn
Composition completed on February 15, 1924. The piece was first performed on April 29, 1924 at the New Century Club, West Chester, Pennsylvania. Barber and his mother, Daisy, were the performers. It is evident that Barber is immersed in discoveries about style and form. Besides his unfinished opera, this fantasie is his largest scale work to date. Barber captures Haydn's style, but expands past it, echoing Beethoven and beyond. Barber used "Josef" as his spelling; "Joseph" is currently preferred

internationally. Previously unpublished. Manuscript source: Library of Congress. An introduction written by the young composer, showing a charming balance of naiveté, pride of accomplishment and a creator's self-awareness, appears in the manuscript, below. "Mrs. Kerlin" was the wife of local poet Robert T. Kerlin, who taught English at West Chester State Teacher's College. Both husband and wife encouraged the young composer's work.[1]

THE LIFE OF THE FANTASIE

The Fantasie was composed, rather completed on Feb. 14, 1924 because of a request by Mrs. Kerlin for a two-piano piece. Completed, I say, because its history went back to an earlier date than that. As far as I can tell, the "Andante con moto" theme was composed in 1920 for one piano. I looked at it later in 1922 with the idea of arranging it for violin, cello and piano. Hence why we still call it the "Trio." But it never worked out. I had then the old theme and the introduction to the B flat part — the little counterpoint, written sometime before, but I was at loss to find the B flat section and so let the thing drop. In January '24, I found it again and finally, about February first, wrote the first section and the B flat major, from which the introduction is constructed.

I wrote the second piano part out one Sunday morning, and Mrs. Kerlin and I played it that afternoon on Mr. Green's Two Pianos. Everyone was much impressed and Mother cried a little for lack of something better to do. I was then thirteen years old.

It was first publicly performed at the New Century Club, April 29, with Mother and I playing it on two specially tuned pianos, a Steinway Grand and an Upright. We had to repeat it.

I like it for its simplicity — it was written in the style of Haydn — and Uncle Sid Homer says it is the best thing I have done!

September 23, 1924

Prelude to a Tragic Drama
Composed in January, 1925. Jeanne Behrend, Curtis classmate of Barber's, recalled that this piece was written for a melodramatic skit of some kind.[2] The excesses of the piece were undoubtedly deliberate. One can sense Barber's glee at discovering and using all sorts of colorful harmonies. Even though the composition is rather tongue in cheek in nature, Barber's development as a pianist and as a composer for piano is obviously moving at a faster pace, comparing this piece with the *Three Sketches* written at age 13. Previously unpublished. Manuscript source: Library of Congress.

Fresh From West Chester (Some Jazzings)
The music is more straightforward than the jokes in the titles and score markings imply.
In the mid-1920s the word "jazz" did not have the specific meaning it later acquired. It was a buzz word of the period, describing something hip, casual and distinctively American. Barber's attempts at jest in the titles, tempo markings and indications may have been his way of concealing any compositional pretense and ambitions for these works in the early period of his studies with Scalero, who apparently did not approve of these two pieces. As compositions they have considerable charm and spontaneous freshness. They display compositional clarity, growing sophistication, and a deepening pianistic sense. Previously unpublished. Manuscript source: Library of Congress.

I. Poison Ivy
Composed in July, 1925. On the cover of the manuscript Barber wrote, "A country-dance that isn't. Accredited to, and blamed on T.T. Garboriasky" (apparently a made-up name). Barber scholar Barbara Heyman cites a story of Barber playing the then untitled first piece for the organist at Westminster Presbyterian Church in West Chester, who breezily suggested the title "Poison Ivy."[2]

II. Let's Sit It Out; I'd Rather Watch; A Walls
Composed in May, 1926. "A Walls" was Barber's jokey and rather awkward reference to a waltz. On the cover of the manuscript the composer wrote, "I, Sam Barber, did it with my little hatchet." At the end of the manuscript Barber wrote, "Soon to be released—Curtis Institute Blues—The Piece that makes People Pray." This was probably a joke; the "Curtis Institute Blues" may have never been composed. In his diary entry of March 11, 1927 Barber wrote, "Piano lesson at 9:30. I played her some of my compositions. She likes the Walls and told me to ask Scalero if I could play it at a pupil's recital. I asked him and he said no."

To Aunt Maime on Her Birthday
Manuscript dated June 19, 1926. Barber scholar Barbara Heyman speculates that "Aunt Maime" (or "Mamie," as she spells it; the manuscript shows "Maime") may have been a family friend.[2] Whoever she was, Barber's feelings for her are apparent in this sentimental and songlike piece. Previously unpublished. Manuscript source: Library of Congress.

Three Essays
By the age of 16 Barber's growing sophistication as a composer, and by implication as a pianist, is unmistakable. These *Essays* are his most ambitious and expansive compositions to date. These early summer pieces appear to have been written for no particular reason or occasion, other than perhaps to celebrate the time that could be allowed to composition after the end of the school year. They show compositional discipline in development of thematic material, even at the risk of repetition. In their free form they vaguely foreshadow his later *Essays* for orchestra. Barber's compositional progress in them is remarkable. In these *Essays* are sounds of the mature composer. He was still wrestling with extended, free form. Previously unpublished. Manuscript source: Library of Congress.

Essay I for Piano
Manuscript dated June 5, 1926. The insistent half step octaves at forte, from the middle section, are later echoed in a Barber choral piece, *Anthony O'Daly*.

Essay II for Piano
Manuscript dated July, 1926. Barber's manuscript is titled "Second Essay for Piano." For the sake of consistency, it is published here with the title "Essay II."

Essay III for Piano
Manuscript dated June, 1926.

Two Interludes
Barber initially used the title Intermezzo for these two pieces. They are listed as "Two Intermezzi for Piano" in a Curtis Institute of Music recital program of May 12, 1932, with the composer as pianist. His *Dover Beach* was premiered on the same evening.[2] Barber's pianist friend Jeanne Behrend performed the two pieces, by now using Barber's revised title of Interludes, on March 1, 1934, at the Philadelphia Academy of Music, and again performed them in 1939 in Philadelphia and New York.[2] Barber originally cited these as Op. 4 on a list of works he wrote in 1978, but later crossed them off. Brahms is the obvious compositional model for these two pieces. Though his composition teacher, Scalero, liked them, perhaps there was a little too much Brahms in them for Barber to feel they belonged among his acknowledged works.

Interlude I
Manuscript dated December 15, 1931. Previously published in Samuel Barber: *Complete Piano Music* (G. Schirmer, 1993).

Interlude II
Manuscript dated January 6, 1932. Previously unpublished.

CHILDHOOD COMPOSITIONS

Facsimiles of the composer's manuscripts of the following childhood piano compositions are included in this collection. Barber did not later acknowledge the boyhood opus numbers given to these early compositions. Previously unpublished, except as noted.

Sadness
"Op. I, No. I." Composed on July 8, 1917. Barber cited this as his first composition. The manuscript shown in facsimile, in Barber's hand, was probably a copy written out a couple of years after composition. The surprising D Major harmony in measure ten points to Barber's improvisation and experimentation at the piano. Though not explicitly stated, Barber probably intended a return to the beginning after the 6/8 section, with a *Fine* at the double bar, line 3. It is interesting that the melancholy which was so often present in Barber's later life and music appears in his very first composition. Manuscript source: Library of Congress.

Melody in F

"Op. I, No. III." Composed in December, 1917. The piece seems to imitate sentimental parlor music of the day and decades before it. Even so, it shows precocious sensitivity for a seven year old composer. Putting the melody in the left hand is inventive for one so young. It also has an obvious vocal quality to the melody, a characteristic of Barber's music in general. (Barber composed his first song, "Sometime," in October, between the composition of "Sadness" and "Melody in F.") Like its predecessor, "Sadness," "Melody in F" includes a contrasting middle section in 6/8, probably modeled on something Barber had heard and liked. Manuscript source: Library of Congress.

Largo

"Op. I, No. IV." Composed in 1918. We do not know the month of composition, but when compared to the more elementary pieces of 1917 it is apparent that Barber is quickly gaining compositional confidence and vocabulary. This "Largo" still shows melody as a dominating element, but has more expansive design and harmonic movement. In the left hand arpeggios at the key change we have Barber's first idiomatic pianistic figure. The composer may have intended a return to the beginning section in C Major after the F Major section. The facsimile manuscript is in Barber's hand, recopied a few years after composition. Manuscript source: Library of Congress.

War Song

"Op. I, No. V." Composed in 1918. We do not know the month of composition, but it is certainly before Armistice Day (November 11), which ended World War I. The use of 3/2 shows inventiveness for an inexperienced and young creator. Barber is obviously attempting as much profundity as he could muster as an eight year old reacting to war. Though no dynamics are indicated, one can guess that he played the opening section loudly. Like the previous early piano pieces, this includes a middle section in contrasting meter. Barber probably had various models for this compositional design. The facsimile was previously published in *Samuel Barber: The Composer and His Music* by Barbara Heyman, Oxford University Press, 1992. Manuscript source: Library of Congress.

At Twilight

"Op. III, No. I." Composed in 1919. There are some obvious mistakes in the manuscript (missing accidentals, misalignment of right and left hands). Barber again seems to be imitating the kind of sentimental song that was popular some years before 1919, but there are also hints that he might have been playing Schumann piano music in this same period. Sam played this piece in a recital presented by students of his piano teacher, William Hatton Green, on June 23, 1919, and again in the same situation in April of 1920.[2] Manuscript source: Library of Congress.

Lullaby

"Op. III, No. II." Composed in 1919. "Dedicated to Daddy." As a composer Barber seems completely distracted by the crossing of hands. Except for that device the piece is harmonically and melodically pedestrian compared to its predecessors. There are some obvious errors in the manuscript. Paired with "At Twilight," "Lullaby" was played on student piano recitals of June 23, 1919 and April 1920.[2] Manuscript source: Library of Congress.

[1] Barbara Heyman, *Samuel Barber: The Composer and His Music* (New York, NY: Oxford University Press, 1992)

[2] Barbara Heyman, *A Comprehensive Thematic Catalog of the Works of Samuel Barber* (New York, NY: Oxford University Press, manuscript copy consulted prior to publication)

[3] Paul Wittke, introduction to *Samuel Barber: Complete Piano Music* (New York, NY: G. Schirmer, Inc., 1984, 1993)

Themes

I. Menuetto

Samuel Barber
April, 1923

II. Andante Religioso

Samuel Barber
1923

III. Allegretto on C

Samuel Barber
1923

Allegro ma non troppo

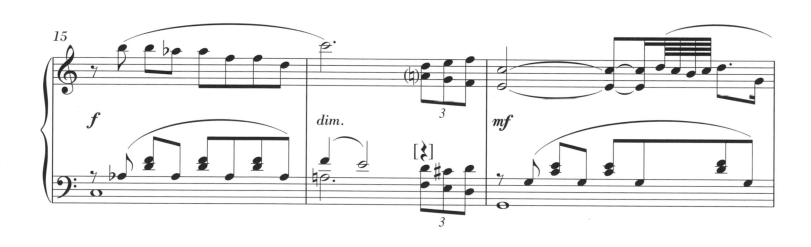

To Jean
Petite Berceuse

Samuel Barber
*c.*1923

Moderato con espressione

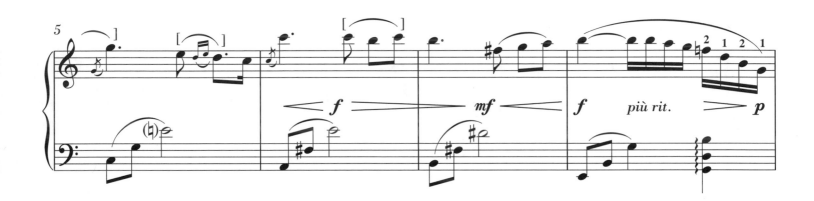

The fingerings are Barber's.

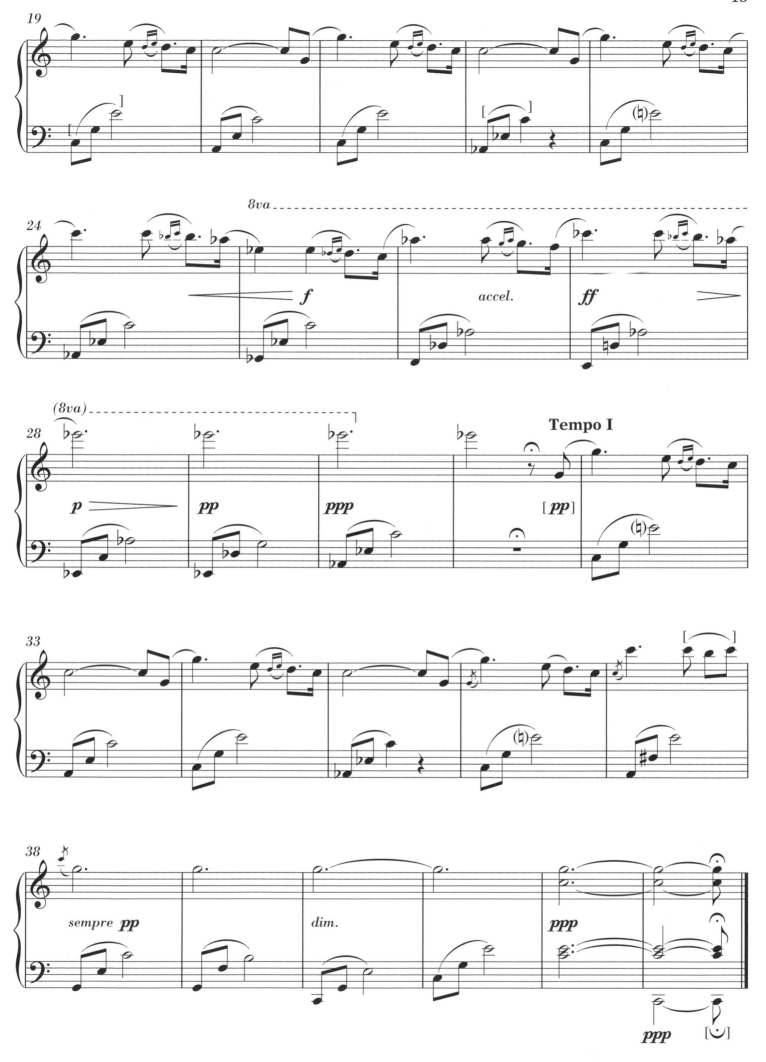

To Mother

Three Sketches
I. Love Song

Samuel Barber
April, 1924

To Number 220601

II. To My Steinway

Samuel Barber
June, 1923

To Sara

III. Minuet

Samuel Barber
April, 1923

*Small-sized notes are original in the private edition of 1923.

**Theme from Beethoven.

*Barber did not indicate staccato in the L.H. eighth notes of this figure although that may have been his intention.

Fantasie for Two Pianos
Written in the Style of Josef Haydn

Samuel Barber
February, 1924

*The manuscript indicates C, D, E for the second and third beats of measure 9. We have chosen to match measure 3.

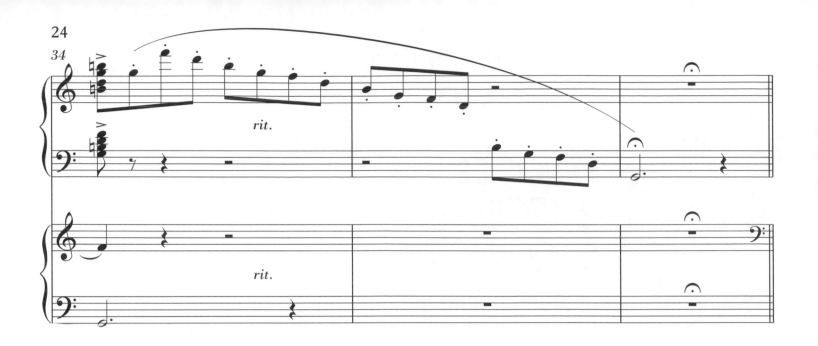

Andante con moto

Tempo di marcia, allegretto

*In the manuscript, the last diad in the left hand of measure 84 is written A–F. This is likely an error given the prevalence of octaves in this section.

**The manuscript indicates two eighth notes on the last beat of measure 88 in the left hand. The pattern would suggest dotted-eighth, sixteenth.

Tempo I

Prelude to a Tragic Drama

Samuel Barber
January, 1925

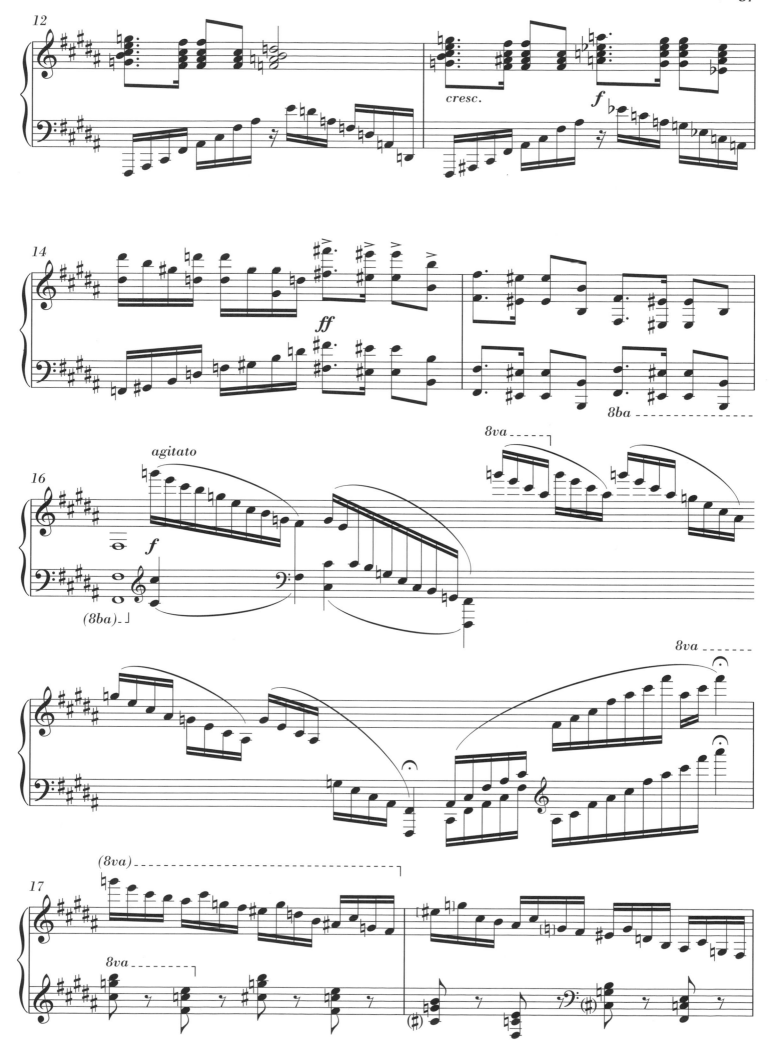

*The manuscript indicates A-sharp and F-sharp; this is likely an error, here corrected.

*The left hand of measure 38 was left incomplete. We have added a likely suggestion based on similar material in measure 12.

lentissimo, ponderoso

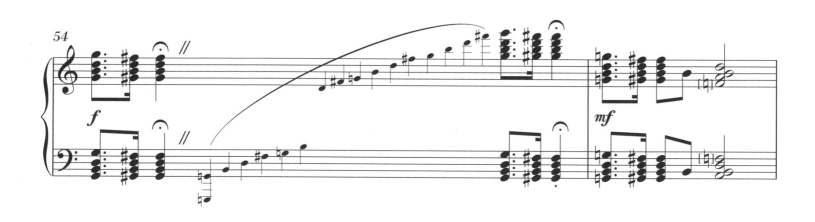

Fresh from West Chester
(Some Jazzings)

I. Poison Ivy

Samuel Barber
July, 1925

Allegro, as a dog wags his tail

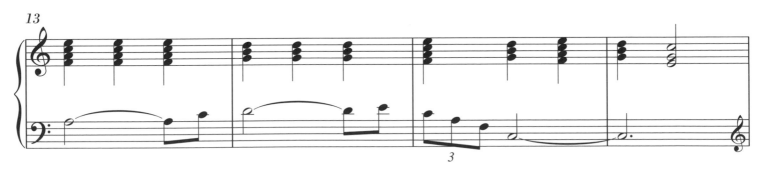

On the cover of the manuscript Barber wrote: "A country-dance that isn't. Accredited to, and blamed on T.T. Garboriasky —July 1925."

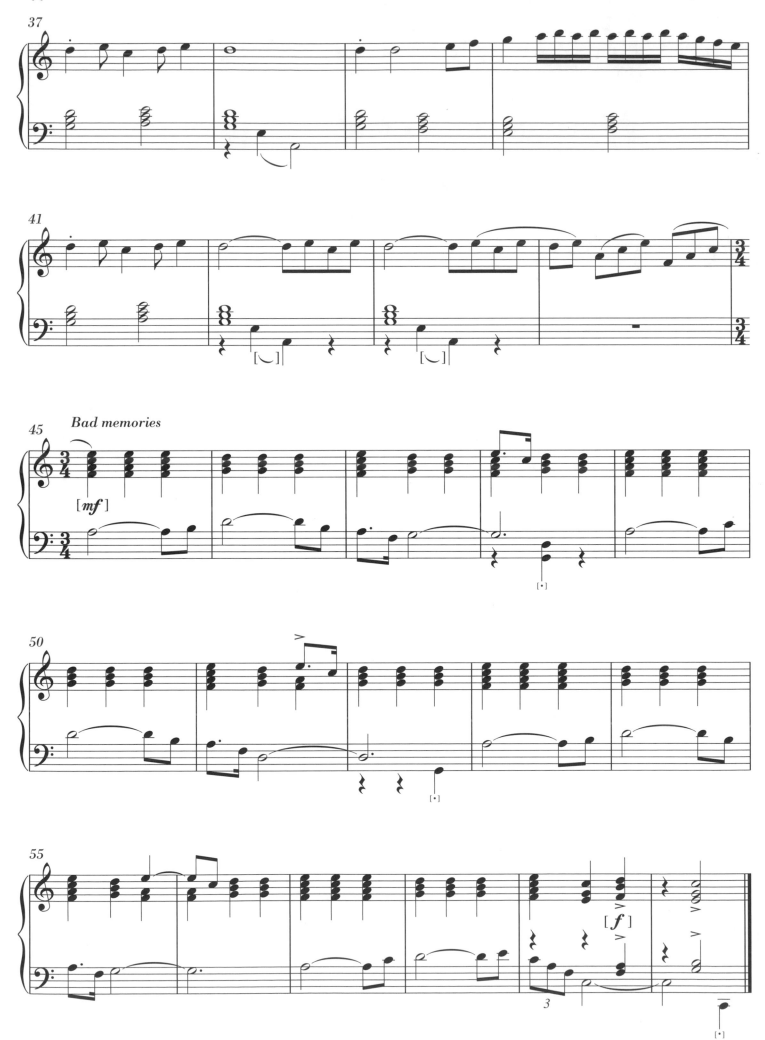

II. Let's Sit It Out; I'd Rather Watch
A Walls*

Samuel Barber
May, 1926

On the cover of the manuscript, Barber wrote: "I, Sam Barber, did it with my little hatchet—May, 1926."

* "A Walls" is a play on the word "waltz."

**Barber indicated few dynamics in this piece. We have made minimal suggestions.

***The manuscript has F3 and A3 on the second and third beats of the left hand diad; editorial choice is to match measure 89, where the manuscript clearly has F and B.

flirtatiously, molto koketto[*]

*Barber made up this word.

*Barber's manuscript indicates a low G natural on the downbeat of measure 80. We believe this to be a mistake, and have matched measure 51. Another discrepancy in the same measure, right hand, has been corrected to match measure 51.

Tempo I

*This mysterious indication appears thus in the manuscript. In an alternate copy of this movement owned by the late Paul Wittke, Barber's editor at G. Schirmer, the direction "pound keys" appears after *(lb)*. It is unclear if the words were added by Wittke or Barber.

At the end of the manuscript Barber wrote: "Soon to be released—*Curtis Institute Blues—The Piece that makes People Pray*."

To Aunt Maime on Her Birthday

Samuel Barber
June 19, 1926

*The word "tranquillo" is a guess at the unintelligible word following "Andante" in the manuscript.

Essay I
for Piano

Samuel Barber
completed June 5, 1926

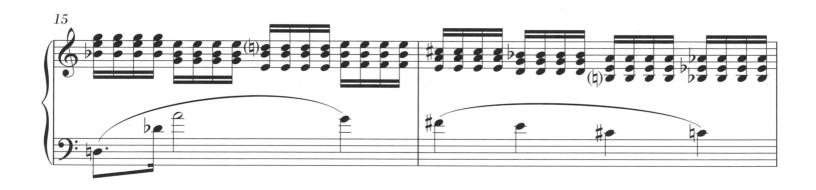

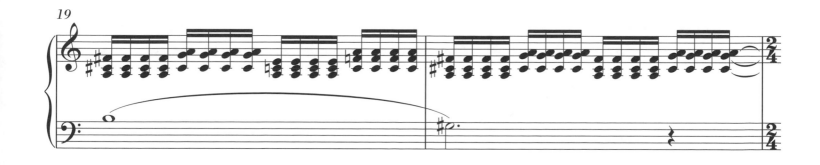

*Barber indicated a quarter note in the right hand on beat two of this measure. As no corresponding note appears in the left hand, no accent appears on the note, and the pattern remains consistent to this point, the editors have omitted the note.

*The low note F-sharp is an editorial guess. No ♯ appears before the low F in the manuscript, nor does a ♮. If Barber had intended a ♮ in this context, we reckon that he would have deliberately indicated it.

Essay II
for Piano

Samuel Barber
July, 1926

Allegro molto

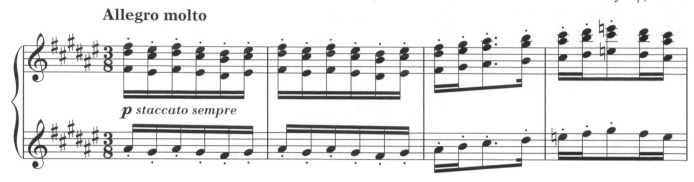

*Barber clearly indicated E-natural in his manuscript when this material later recurs.
**The pattern would suggest the note F-sharp in the left hand; Barber's manuscript has G-sharp.

*Barber's manuscript indicates a B-natural in the left hand chord. We believe this is an error and have matched measure 127.

*This chord is written as a quarter note in the manuscript, likely an error.

**The left hand of this measure is written an octave higher in the manuscript. Barber writes "8va bassa" below. We have notated it as such, an octave lower. Because of context, we assume this refers only to measure 51.

*The manuscript is unclear on the second figure in the left hand. Printed is our best guess of Barber's intention.
**"Lenápe"—a region of the country largely in Delaware, New Jersey, New York, and Pennsylvania named for the Lenape Indian tribe that inhabited this area, a likely reference to Lake Lenape Park, a local weekend get-away spot about 40 miles north of where Barber grew up.

Essay III
for Piano

Samuel Barber
completed June 30, 1926

Con moto
the theme with monotonous emphasis throughout

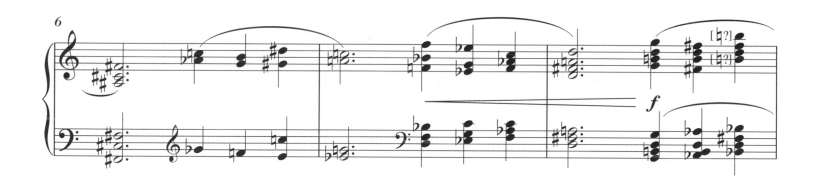

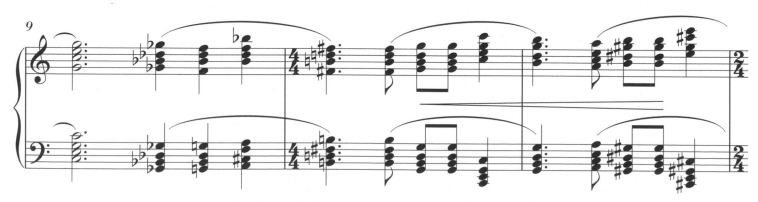

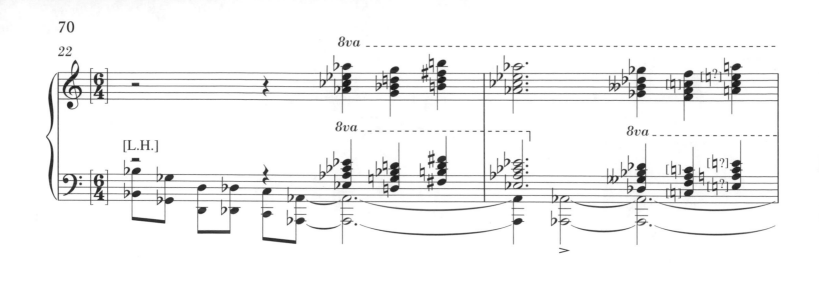

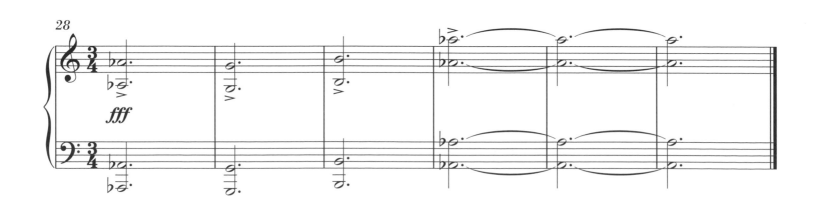

Interlude I

Samuel Barber
completed December 15, 1931

Interlude II

Samuel Barber
completed January 6, 1932

*The metronome marking is unclear on the manuscript. It may be interpreted as ♩ = 160 or ♩. = 160.
The latter seems impossibly fast.

**Over the fifth eighth note in measure 12 Barber indicates *f*, followed by *p* over the downbeat of measure 13. These
dynamics conflict with those under the staff, and were editorially omitted. There are no manuscript dynamics when the
same material later recurs.

*Measure 102 in Barber's manuscript, the counterpart to this measure, has an alternate inversion of this chord.

**When this material recurs, it is articulated thus: ♩♪ This may have been deliberate, but it is more likely an oversight.

Più mosso e leggiero

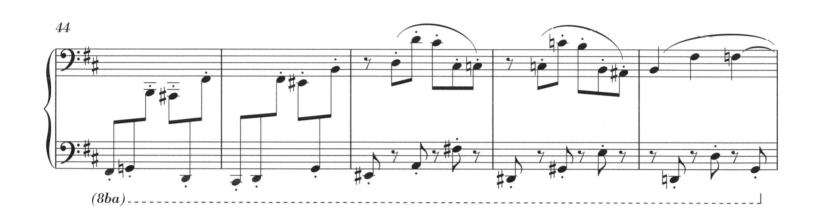

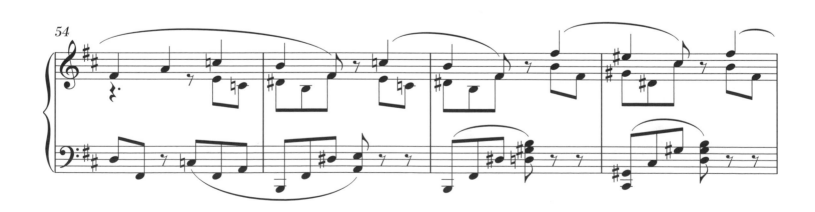

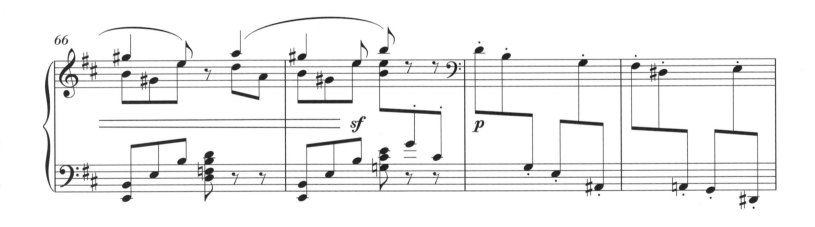

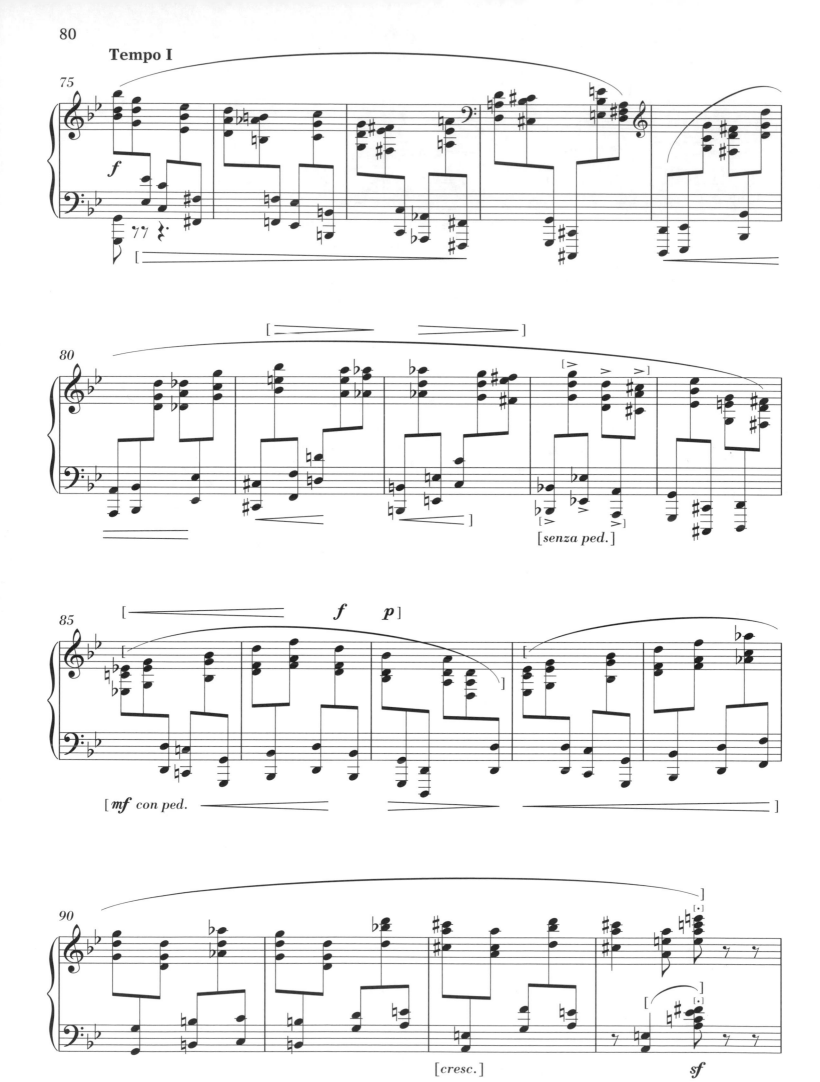

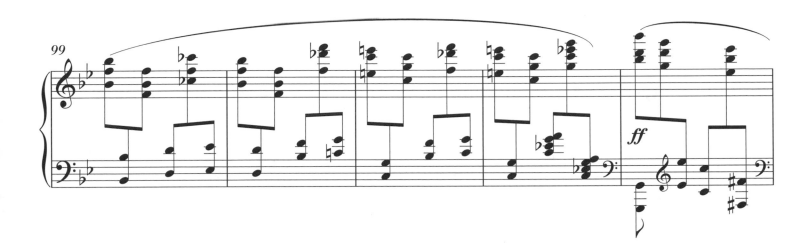

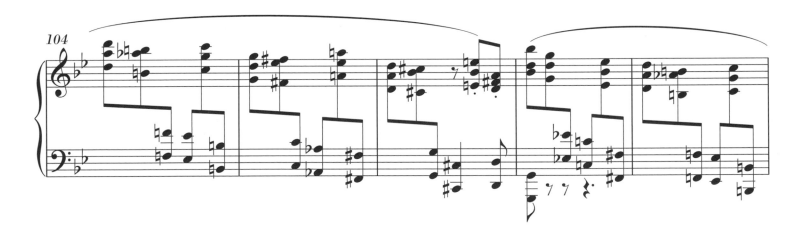

MANUSCRIPT FACSIMILES OF CHILDHOOD COMPOSITIONS

AT TWILIGHT